Devotion to the Sacred Heart

Compiled by the Daughters of St. Paul

Pauline

BOOKS & MEDIA

Boston

ISBN 0-8198-1858-5

Second edition, based on the 1991 edition of the *Queen of Apostles Prayerbook,* Pauline Books & Media.

Printed and published in the U.S.A. by Pauline Books & Media, 50 St. Paul's Avenue, Boston, MA 02130.

http://www.pauline.org

Pauline Books & Media is the publishing house of the Daughters of St. Paul, an international congregation of women religious serving the Church with the communications media.

Contents

Prayers to the Sacred Heart

Morning Offering of the Apostleship of Prayer

O Jesus, through the Immaculate Heart of Mary, I offer you all my prayers, works, joys and sufferings of this day, for the intentions of your Sacred Heart, in union with the holy sacrifice of the Mass throughout the world, in reparation for my sins, for the intentions of all our associates and for the general intention recommended this month.

Aspiration by St. Margaret Mary

O heart of love, I place my trust entirely in you. Though I fear all things from my weakness, I hope all things from your goodness!

Thanksgiving for the Eucharist

Jesus, Divine Master, I thank and bless your most lovable heart for the great gift of the Holy Eucharist. Your love makes you dwell in the tabernacle, renew your passion in the Mass and give yourself as food for our souls in holy Communion.

May I know you, O hidden God! May I draw life-giving waters from the font of your heart. Grant me the grace to visit you every day in this sacrament, to understand and actively participate in holy Mass, to receive holy Communion often and with the right dispositions.

Thanksgiving for the Church

Jesus, Divine Master, I bless and thank your most gentle heart for the great gift of the Church. She is the Mother who instructs us in the truth, guides us on the way to heaven and communicates supernatural life to us. She continues your own saving mission here on earth, as your Mystical Body. She is the ark of salvation. She is infallible, indefectible, catholic. Grant me the grace to love the Church as you loved her and sanctified her in your blood. May the world know her, may all sheep enter her fold, may everyone humbly cooperate in your kingdom.

Thanksgiving for the Priesthood

Jesus, Divine Master, I bless and thank your most loving heart for the institution of the priesthood. Priests are sent by you, as you were sent by the Father. To them you entrusted the treasures of your doctrine, of your law, of your grace and God's people themselves. Grant me the grace to love your priests, listen to them and let myself be guided by them in your ways. Send good laborers into your vineyard, Jesus. May priests be the salt that purifies and preserves; may they be the light of the world. May they be the city placed on the mountain. May they all be formed according to your heart. And one day in heaven may they have around themselves, as a crown of joy, a great throng of souls won for you.

Thanksgiving for the Religious State

Jesus, Divine Master, I thank and bless your most holy heart for the institution of the religious state. As in heaven, so also on earth the mansions are many. You have chosen those whom you wish to follow you in religious life and you have called them to evangelical perfection. You have made yourself their model, their help and their reward. Divine Heart, multiply religious vocations. Sustain them in faithful observance of the evangelical counsels. May they adorn your Church with virtue. May they console you, pray and work for your honor in every apostolate.

Thanksgiving for Mary, Our Mother

Jesus, Divine Master, I thank and bless your most merciful heart for having given us Mary most holy as our Mother, Teacher and Queen. From the cross you placed us all in her hands. You gave her a great heart, much wisdom and immense power. May everyone know her, love her, pray to her. May all permit themselves to be led by her to you, the Savior of the world. I place myself in her hands, as you placed yourself. With this Mother I want to live now, in the hour of my death and for all eternity.

Thanksgiving for the Passion of Jesus

Jesus, Divine Master, I thank and bless your most gentle heart, which led you to give your life for me. Your blood, your wounds, the scourges, the thorns, the cross, your bowed head tell me: "No one loves more than he who gives his life for the loved one." The shepherd died to give life to the sheep. I too want to spend my life for you. May you always, everywhere and in all things dispose of me for your greater glory. May I always repeat: "Your will be done." Inflame my heart with holy love for you and for everyone.

The Nine First Fridays

The writings of St. Margaret Mary mention many promises that the Sacred Heart of Jesus has made in favor of his devoted ones. The principal promises are:

1. I will give them all the graces necessary for their state of life.

2. I will give peace in their families.

3. I will console them in all their troubles.

4. I will be their refuge in life and especially in death.

5. I will abundantly bless all their undertakings.

6. Sinners will find in my heart the source and infinite ocean of mercy.

7. Tepid souls will become fervent.

8. Fervent souls will rise speedily to great perfection.

9. I will bless those places where the image of my Sacred Heart shall be exposed and venerated.

10. I will give priests the power to touch the most hardened hearts.

11. Persons who propagate this devotion will have their names eternally written in my heart.

12. In the abundant mercy of my heart, I promise that my all-powerful love will grant to all those who will receive Communion on the first Fridays of nine consecutive months the grace of final repentance. They will not die in my displeasure, nor without receiving the sacraments, and my heart will be their secure refuge in that last hour.

Conditions required:

1. To make nine holy Communions;

2. on the first Friday of the month;

3. for nine consecutive months, without interruption;

4. with the proper disposition;

5. with the intention of making reparation to the Sacred Heart of Jesus and to obtain the fruit of this great promise.

Act of Reparation to
the Most Sacred Heart of Jesus

A partial indulgence is granted to the faithful who devoutly recite this act of reparation. A plenary indulgence (with the usual conditions) is granted if it is publicly recited on the feast of the Most Sacred Heart of Jesus.

O most loving Jesus, whose immense love for humanity is repaid by so much forgetfulness, negligence and contempt, see us kneeling before your altar. We wish to make a special act of homage in reparation for the indifference and injuries to which your loving heart is everywhere subjected.

We ourselves have taken part in this ill-treatment, and we regret it now from the depths of our hearts. We humbly ask your pardon and declare our readiness to atone by voluntary penance not only for our personal offenses, but also for the sins of those who have strayed from the path of salvation.

We want to atone for those who obstinately refuse to follow you, their shepherd and leader. We want to atone for those who even renounce the vows of their Baptism and cast off the easy yoke of your law.

While we intend to expiate all such sins, we propose to make reparation for each one in particular:

—immodesty in dress and actions,

—the many seductions that ensnare the innocent,

 —the violation of Sundays and holydays,

 —the blasphemies spoken against you and your saints,

 —the insults hurled against your Vicar and your priests,

 —the negligence and the sacrileges by which the very sacrament of your love is profaned,

 —and finally the public crimes of all nations who resist the rights and the teaching authority of the Church you have founded.

If only we could wash away such sins with our blood! And now, in reparation for these violations of your divine honor, we offer the satisfaction that you once made on the cross to your Father, which you renew daily on our altars. We offer it in union with the expiation of your Virgin Mother, all the saints and the faithful on earth. With the help of your grace, we promise to make reparation, as much as we are able, for the neglect of your great love and for the sins that we and others have committed in the past. We intend to do this by a firm faith, an innocent life and the observance of the law of charity. We promise to prevent others with all our powers from offending you and to bring as many as possible to follow you.

O loving Jesus, through the intercession of the Blessed Virgin Mary, our model in reparation, accept our voluntary offering of this act of reparation. By the crowning gift of perseverance, keep us faithful until death in our duty and in the allegiance we owe to you, so that one day we may all come to that happy home where you, with the Father and the Holy Spirit, live and reign, God, forever and ever. Amen.

A partial indulgence is granted to the faithful who devoutly recite the above Act of Reparation. A plenary indulgence is granted (under the usual conditions) if it is publicly recited on the feast of the Most Sacred Heart of Jesus.

Act of Consecration to the Most Sacred Heart of Jesus

Most loving Jesus, Redeemer of the human race, look on us kneeling humbly before your altar. We are yours, and yours we wish to be. But to be more surely united to you, we freely consecrate ourselves today to your most Sacred Heart. Many people have never known you. Many, too, scorning your precepts, have rejected you.

Have mercy on them all, most merciful Jesus, and draw them to your Sacred Heart.

Be king, O Lord, not only of the faithful who have never forsaken you, but also of the prodigal children who have abandoned you. Grant that they may quickly return to their Father's house.

Lord, grant to your Church freedom and immunity from harm. Give peace and order to all nations. Make the earth resound from pole to pole with one cry: Praise to the divine heart that wrought our salvation. To Jesus Christ be glory and honor forever. Amen.

Consecration of the Family
to the Sacred Heart

The consecration of the family to the Sacred Heart is a devotion desired by our Lord, who has promised to bless families consecrated to him. "I will bless," he said, "those homes where an image of my heart shall be exposed and venerated. I shall give peace in their families. I shall abundantly bless all their undertakings. I shall be their secure refuge in life and especially at the hour of death."

In order to make this consecration, one must have a representation of the Sacred Heart of Jesus that has been blessed by a priest. After the image has been set in a place of honor, the consecration of the entire family is made.

Jesus has granted many favors, even extraordinary ones, to those families which have received him into their midst by consecrating themselves to his Sacred Heart. Among the graces may be mentioned help received in critical periods, dangers averted and discords settled. Above all, countless persons have returned to the Faith.

Act of Consecration of the Family to the Sacred Heart

O most loving heart of Jesus, who gave St. Margaret Mary this consoling promise, "I will bless those homes in which an image of my Sacred Heart shall be exposed and venerated," we ask you to accept today the consecration of our family to you. By this act we intend to solemnly proclaim the dominion that you have over all creatures and over us, recognizing you as our king. Some refuse to acknowledge your dominion and repeat the cry: "We do not want this one to reign over us," thus offending your most loving heart. We, on the other hand, repeat with greater fervor and more ardent love: O Jesus, reign over our family and over each of its members. Reign over our minds, that we may always believe in the truths you have taught us. Reign over our hearts, that we may always follow your divine teachings. O divine heart, you alone are our loving king. You have purchased us with your precious blood.

And now keep your promise and let your blessings fall on us. Bless us in our labors, in our undertakings, in our health, in our interests. Bless us in joy and in sorrow, in prosperity and in adversity, now and always. Grant that peace may reign in our midst, as well as harmony, respect, love for one another and good example.

Defend us from dangers, from sickness, from accidents and, above all, from sin. Finally, write our names in your Sacred Heart, and grant that they may always remain there, so that after having been united with you on earth, we may one day be united with you in heaven, to sing the glories and the triumphs of your mercy. Amen.

Aspiration: We want God, who is our Father; we want God, who is our king.

Now recite one Our Father, one Hail Mary and one Glory to the Father, in honor of the Sacred Heart of Jesus, and a Hail, Holy Queen to the Blessed Virgin Mary to obtain her protection.

It is fitting to renew this consecration on great feasts of our Lord, such as Christmas, Easter and Corpus Christi.

Prayer to the Sacred Heart of Jesus

To be said before each action

Adorable heart, in all you have done and suffered on earth, you have sought the glory of the heavenly Father and the accomplishment of his holy will. Grant that in union with you, I may offer him the action I am about to begin, with the sole desire of pleasing him and doing his will. Grant me the grace to perform it as I ought. Amen.

Litany of the Sacred Heart of Jesus

Lord, have mercy on us.
Christ, have mercy on us.
Lord, have mercy on us.
Christ, hear us.
Christ, graciously hear us.
God, the Father of heaven, have mercy on us.
God the Son, Redeemer of the world,*
God the Holy Spirit,
Holy Trinity, one God,
Heart of Jesus, formed by the Holy Spirit in the
    womb of the Virgin Mother,
Heart of Jesus, substantially united
        to the Word of God,
Heart of Jesus, of infinite majesty,
Heart of Jesus, sacred temple of God,
Heart of Jesus, tabernacle of the Most High,
Heart of Jesus, burning furnace of charity,
Heart of Jesus, abode of justice and love,
Heart of Jesus, full of goodness and love,
Heart of Jesus, source of all virtues,
Heart of Jesus, most worthy of all praise,
Heart of Jesus, king and center of all hearts,
Heart of Jesus, in whom are all the treasures of
    wisdom and knowledge,
Heart of Jesus, in whom dwells
        the fullness of divinity,

Have mercy on us.

Heart of Jesus, in whom the Father
	was well pleased,
Heart of Jesus, of whose fullness
	we have all received,
Heart of Jesus, desire of the everlasting hills,
Heart of Jesus, patient and most merciful,
Heart of Jesus, enriching all who invoke you,
Heart of Jesus, fountain of life and holiness,
Heart of Jesus, propitiation for our sins,
Heart of Jesus, laden with insults,
Heart of Jesus, bruised for our offenses,
Heart of Jesus, obedient unto death,
Heart of Jesus, pierced with a lance,
Heart of Jesus, source of all consolation,
Heart of Jesus, our life and resurrection,
Heart of Jesus, our peace and reconciliation,
Heart of Jesus, victim for sins,
Heart of Jesus, salvation of those who trust in you,
Heart of Jesus, hope of those who die in you,
Heart of Jesus, delight of all the saints,

Lamb of God, you take away the sins of the world, spare us, O Lord.

Lamb of God, you take away the sins of the world, graciously hear us, O Lord.

Lamb of God, you take away the sins of the world, have mercy on us.

V. Jesus, gentle and humble of heart,

R. Make our hearts like yours.

Let us pray. Almighty and eternal God, look upon the heart of your beloved Son. Behold the praise and satisfaction he offers you in the name of sinners and for all who seek your mercy. Grant us pardon in the name of the same Jesus Christ, your Son, who lives and reigns with you in the unity of the Holy Spirit forever and ever. Amen.